A Way of Life (Annotated)
An address delivered to Yale students

By Sir William Osler
Annotated by Eddie Merkel

Cover design and forward to this version
Copyright © 2016 by Eddie Merkel

For my grandfather

Original Foreward

In the spring of 1913 Osler came to the United States to deliver the Silliman Lectures at Yale University. Before coming he had promised to give a talk to the students and it is this "lay sermon" which is here reprinted. Cushing[1] in his "Life of Osler" directs attention to the pressure under which it was written, although there is no evidence of any effort in its finish. He quotes from a note written by Osler on the original manuscript, "I wrote this on the steamer going to America, from notes that I had been jotting down for a month, but I only finished it on the Sunday of its delivery," and Cushing adds that on the Saturday before he read the address Osler buried himself in the Graduates' Club at New Haven to complete his task, and that "the last seven of the nineteen pages of the manuscript from which he read, and from which the address was printed, are hand-written on paper of the Graduates" Club of New Haven."

The gist of Osler's sermon is a plea to do the day's work, to live in the day, and he tells how when a very young man he read Carlyle's familiar dictum: "Our business is not to see what lies dimly at a distance, but to do what lies clearly at hand."

Cushing says that in a copy of the address in Osler's library the author had inscribed the following poem:

> "Listen to the Exhortation of the Dawn!
> Look to this Day!
> For it is Life, the very Life of Life.
> In its brief Course lie all the
> Varieties and Realities of your Existence:
> The Bliss of Growth,
> The Glory of Action,
> The Splendour of Beauty;
> For Yesterday is but a Dream
> And Tomorrow is only a Vision;
> But Today well lived makes
> Every Yesterday a Dream of Happiness,
> And every Tomorrow a Vision of Hope.
> Look well therefore to this Day!
> Such is the Salutation of the Dawn!"

Beneath the poem Osler had written "If another reprint is called for put this on this page." We gladly comply with Sir William's suggestion that such an exquisite bit of verse should be recalled.

A Way of Life (Annotated)
Francis R. Packard

---

[1] Harvey Cushing (April 8, 1869 - Oct 7, 1939) American neurosurgeon and a pioneer in brain surgery. Considered one of the "fathers" of neurosurgery.

Forward to this version

I was first introduced to this little book as a teenager by my maternal grandfather. It was important to him and he was important to me, but I just didn't get it at the time. Just as Osler himself says early in this book "*What have bright eyes, red blood, quick breath and taut muscles to do with philosophy?*" A book about living for the day wasn't something that I, as a 16 or 17 year old wanted to hear about at the time. I had all sorts of plans and dreams and ideas for the future.

Later, when my wife and I had our first child, we were over with my grandparents, showing off our new daughter, Sonia. We were getting ready to leave and were out on their drive, putting Sonia in the car. It was a cold, blustery day but my grandparents were both out with us, seeing us off. My grandfather was already looking square in the face of the fact that he had Alzheimer's disease by this time. As we were leaving he handed me our own little copy of the book, inscribed in front to my wife and I from he and my grandmother. As he handed it to me his eyes were pleading with me to listen to him and actually give the book a chance. It was so desperately important to him that I should "get it" that the memory has never faded in my mind.

Many years have passed from that time to now. Sonia is now a grown woman with a son of her own and my grandmother and grandfather are both long gone. Nevertheless, since that time I have read this book regularly, sometimes daily for months at a time. I almost have the entire thing memorized and it is always with me. I have shared it with friends and family. Some people have taken Osler's message in the little book to heart and some have not. It's not something I have followed up with anyone about. Everyone has to make their own way and they don't have to make me happy as long as they make themselves happy. However, a few years ago one person I lent the book to told me that the old fashioned language put him off and because of that he didn't enjoy reading it. I never had a problem with the language but I do agree that some of the examples that he used originally are not as clearly obvious today. To that end I have tried to annotate the text so that the message still comes through and the examples are meaningful to us in this time. What Osler has to say in these few pages is important so I hope my meager additions help you enjoy his message.

The actual text of this version is as it appears in my little copy. I have changed or removed nothing. The only additions I have made are in the form of footnotes and in the appendix.

A Way of Life (Annotated)

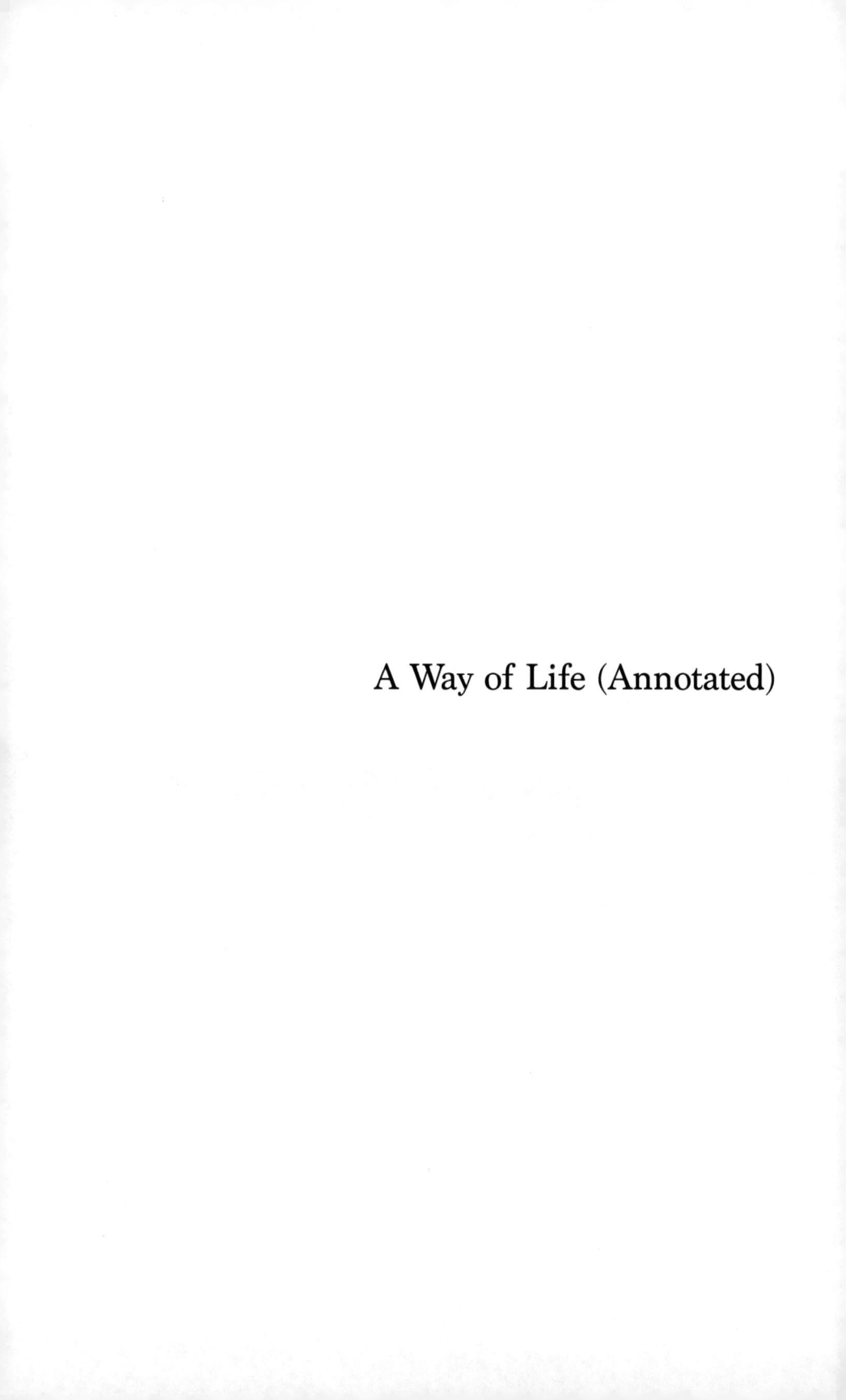

WHAT EACH DAY needs that shalt thou ask,
Each day will set its proper task.

- Goethe

Fellow Students:

Every man has a philosophy of life in thought, in word, or in deed, worked out in himself unconsciously. In possession of the very best, he may not know of its existence; with the very worst he may pride himself as a paragon. As it grows with the growth it cannot be taught to the young in formal lectures. What have bright eyes, red blood, quick breath and taut muscles to do with philosophy? Did not the great Stagirite[1] say that young men were unfit students of it? -- they will hear as though they heard not, and to no profit. Why then should I trouble you? Because I have a message that may be helpful. It is not philosophical, nor is it strictly moral or religious, one or the other of which I was told my address should be, and yet in a way it is all three. It is the oldest and the freshest, the simplest and the most useful, so simple indeed is it that some of you may turn away disappointed as was Naaman the Syrian when told to go wash in Jordan and be clean.[2] You know those composite tools to be bought for 50 cents, with one handle to fit a score or more of instruments. The workmanship is usually bad, so bad, as a rule, that you will not

A Way of Life (Annotated)

find an example in any good carpenter's shop; but the boy has one, the chauffeur slips one into his box, and the sailor into his kit, and there is one in the odds-and-ends drawer of the pantry of every well regulated family. It is simply a handy thing about the house, to help over the many little difficulties of the day. Of this sort of philosophy I wish to make you a present -- a handle to fit your life tools.

Whether the workmanship is Sheffield[3] or shoddy, this helve will fit anything from a hatchet to a corkscrew.

My message is but a word, a Way, an easy expression of the experience of a plain man whose life has never been worried by any philosophy higher than that of the shepherd in As You Like It.[4] I wish to point out a path in which the wayfaring man, though a fool, cannot err; not a system to be worked out painfully only to be discarded, not a formal scheme, simply a habit as easy--or as hard!-- to adopt as any other habit, good or bad.

[1] Aristotle
[2] Luke 4:25-27
[3] According to Wikipedia, during the 19th century Sheffield became prominent internationally for its steel production and innovations like stainless steel.
[4] "As You Like It" is a play by William Shakespeare, thought to have been written in 1599 and first published in 1623.

The shepherd Corin's philosophy is detailed in his speech in Act 3 Scene 2."Sir, I am a true labourer: I earn what I eat, get that I wear, owe no man hate, envy no man's happiness, glad of other men's good, content with my harm, and the greatest of my pride is to see my ewes graze and my lambs suck."

1

A FEW years ago a Xmas card went the rounds, with the legend, *"Life is just one 'derned' thing after another,"* which, in more refined language, is the same as saying, "Life is a habit," a succession of actions that become more or less automatic. This great truth, which lies at the basis of all actions, muscular or psychic, is the keystone to the teaching of Aristotle, to whom the formation of habits was the basis of moral excellence.

> "In a word, habits of any kind are the result of actions of the same kind; and so what we have to do, is to give a certain character to these particular actions" (Ethics).

Lift a seven months old baby to his feet -- see him tumble on his nose. Do the same at twelve months -- he walks. At two years he runs. The muscles and the nervous system have acquired the habit. One trial after another, one failure after another, has given him power. Put your finger in a baby's mouth, and he sucks away in blissful anticipation of a response to a mammalian habit millions of years old. And we can deliberately train parts of our body to perform complicated actions with unerring accuracy. Watch that musician playing a difficult piece. Batteries, commutators, multipliers, switches, wires innumerable control those nimble figures, the machinery of which may be set in motion as automatically as in a pianola, the player all the time chatting as if he had nothing to do in

A Way of Life (Annotated)

controlling the apparatus -- habit again, the gradual acquisition of power by long practice and at the expense of many mistakes. The same great law reaches through mental and moral states. "Character," which partakes of both, in Plutarch's words, is "long-standing habit."

Now the way of life that I preach is a habit to be acquired gradually by long and steady repetition. It is the practice of living for the day only, and for the day's work, Life in day-tight compartments. "Ah," I hear you say, "that is an easy matter, simple as Elisha's advice!"[1] Not as I shall urge it, in words which fail to express the depth of my feelings as to its value. I started life in the best of all environments -- in a parsonage, one of nine children. A man who has filled Chairs in four universities, has written a successful book, and has been asked to lecture at Yale, is supposed popularly to have brains of special quality. A few of my intimate friends really know the truth about me, as I know it! Mine, in good faith I say it, are of the most mediocre character. But what about those professorships, etc.? Just habit, a way of life, an outcome of the day's work, the vital importance of which I wish to impress upon you with all the force at my command.

Dr. Johnson[2] remarked upon the trifling circumstances by which men's lives are influenced, "not by an ascendant planet, a predominating humor, but by the first book which they read, some early conversation which they have heard, or some accident which excited ardor and enthusiasm.[3]" This was my case in two particulars. I was diverted to the Trinity College School, then at Weston, Ontario, by a paragraph in the circular stating that the senior boys would go into the drawing-room in the evenings, and learn to sing and dance -- vocal and pedal accomplishments for which I was never designed; but like Saul seeking his asses[4], I found something more valuable, a man of the White of Selborne[5] type, who knew nature, and who knew how to get boys interested in it. The other happened in the summer of 1871, when I was attending the Montreal General Hospital. Much worried as to the future, partly about the final examination, partly as to what I should do afterwards, I picked up a volume of Carlyle,[6] and on the page I opened there was the familiar sentence --

"Our main business is not to see what lies dimly at a distance, but to do what lies clearly at hand.[7]"

A commonplace sentiment enough, but it hit and stuck and

helped, and was the starting point of a habit that has enabled me to utilize to the full the single talent entrusted to me.

[1] 2 Kings 5:10

"Go, wash yourself seven times in the Jordan, and your flesh will be restored and you will be cleansed."
[2] Dr. Samuel Johnson (1709 - 1784) English poet, essayist, moralist, literary critic, biographer, editor and lexicographer.

A good quote from him that bears on this theme: "The future is purchased by the present"
[3] Moral Essays - The Works of Alexander Pope
[4] 1 Samuel 9

Saul went to look for lost donkeys, but in the end met Samuel and found he was appointed by God to lead all of Israel.
[5] Gilbert White (1720 - 1793) English naturalist
[6] Thomas Carlyle (1795 - 1881) Scottish author, essayist and historian
[7] "Signs of the Times" 1829

2

THE WORKERS in Christ's vineyard were hired by the day;[1] only for this day are we to ask for our daily bread, and we are expressly bidden to take no thought for the morrow. To the modern world these commands have an Oriental savour, counsels of perfection akin to certain of the Beatitudes,[2] stimuli to aspiration, not to action. I am prepared on the contrary to urge the literal acceptance of the advice, not in the mood of St. James -- "Go to now, ye that say, To-day or to-morrow we will go into such a city, and continue there a year, and buy and sell and get gain; whereas ye know not what shall be on the morrow";[3] not in the Epicurean spirit of Omar with his "jug of wine and thou,[4]" but in the modernist spirit, as a way of life, a habit, a strong enchantment at once against the mysticism of the East and the pessimism that too easily besets us. Change that hard saying "sufficient unto the day is the evil thereof,[5]" into "the goodness thereof," since the chief worries of life arise from the foolish habit of looking before and after. As a patient with double vision from some transient unequal action of the muscles of the eye finds magical relief from well-adjusted glasses, so, returning to the clear binocular vision of today, the over-anxious student finds peace when he looks neither backward to the past nor forward to the future.

I stood on the bridge of one of the great liners, ploughing the ocean at 25 knots. "She is alive," said my companion, "in every plate; a huge stomach, with a wonderful heart and lungs, and a splendid

A Way of Life (Annotated)

system of locomotion." Just at that moment a signal sounded, and all over the ship the water-tight compartments were closed. "Our chief factor of safety," said the captain. "In spite of the Titanic," I said. "Yes," he replied, "in spite of the Titanic." Now each one of you is a much more marvelous organization than the great liner, and bound on a longer voyage. What I urge is that you so learn to control the machinery as to live with "day-tight compartments" as the most certain way to ensure safety on the voyage. Get on the bridge and see that at least the great bulkheads are in working order. Touch a button and hear, at every level of your life, the iron doors shutting out the Past -- the dead yesterdays. Touch another and shut off, with a metal curtain, the Future -- the unborn to-morrows. Then you are safe -- safe for to-day! Read the old story in the Chambered Nautilus, [6] so beautifully sung by Oliver Wendell Holmes, only change one line to "Day after day behold the silent toil." Shut off the past. "Let the dead past bury its dead.[7]" So easy to say, so hard to realize! The truth is, the past haunts us like a shadow. To disregard it is not easy. Those blue eyes of your grandmother, that weak chin of your grandfather, have mental and moral counterparts in your make-up. Generations of ancestors, brooding over "Providence, foreknowledge, will and fate, Fixed fate, free will, foreknowledge absolute,[8]" may have bred a New England conscience, morbidly sensitive, to heal which some of you had rather sing the 51st Psalm than follow Christ into the slums. Shut out the yesterdays, which have lighted fools the way to dusty death, and have no concern for you personally, that is consciously. They are there all right, working daily in us, but so are our livers and stomachs. And the past, in its unconscious action on our lives, should bother us as little as they do. The petty annoyances, the real and fancied slights, the trivial mistakes, the disappointments, the sins, the sorrows, even the joys -- bury them deep in the oblivion of each night. Ah! but it is just then that to so many of us the ghosts of the past,

> Night-riding Incubi
> Troubling the fantasy,[9]

come in troops, and pry open the eyelids, each presenting a sin, a sorrow, a regret. Bad enough in the old and seasoned, in the young these demons of past sins may be a terrible affliction, and in bitterness of heart many a one cries with Eugene Aram, "Oh God! Could I so close my mind, and clasp it with a clasp.[10]" As a vaccine against all morbid poisons left in the system by the infections of yesterday, I offer "a way of life." "Undress," as George Herbert[11] says, "your soul at night," not by self-examination, but by shedding, as you do your garments, the daily sins whether of omission or of commission, and you will wake a free man, with a new life. To look back, except on rare occasions for stock-taking, is to risk the fate of Lot's wife.[12] Many a man is handicapped in his course by a cursed combination of retro- and intro-spection, the mistakes of yesterday paralysing the efforts of to-day, the worries of the past hugged to his destruction, and the worm Regret allowed to canker the very heart of his life. To die daily, after the manner of St. Paul, ensures the resurrection of a new man, who makes each day the epitome of life.

[1] Matthew 20:1-16

In this story a wealthy landowner hires workers for his vineyards. Some he hires in the morning and he continues to hire workers all day long. When it comes time to pay the workers the workers who were first hired are upset that the workers hired near the end of the day are paid the same wage that they receive. The landowner argues that he has a right to be generous with his own money. This is where the saying "the last will be first and the first will be last" comes from.
[2] Matthew 5:1-12

"Blessed are the poor in spirit,
  for theirs is the kingdom of heaven.
Blessed are those who mourn,
  for they will be comforted.
Blessed are the meek,
  for they will inherit the earth.
Blessed are those who hunger and thirst   for righteousness,
  for they will be filled.
Blessed are the merciful,
  for they will be shown mercy.
Blessed are the pure in heart,
  for they will see God.
Blessed are the peacemakers,
  for they will be called children of God.
Blessed are those who are persecuted because of righteousness,
  for theirs is the kingdom of heaven.
Blessed are you when people insult you, persecute you and falsely say all kinds of evil against you because of me. Rejoice and be glad, because great is your reward in heaven, for in the same way they persecuted the prophets who were before you."
[3] James 4:13-14

"Now listen, you who say, "Today or tomorrow we will go to this or that city,

A Way of Life (Annotated)

spend a year there, carry on business and make money." 14 Why, you do not even know what will happen tomorrow. What is your life? You are a mist that appears for a little while and then vanishes."

[4] Rubaiyat of Omar Khayyam
[5] Matthew 6:34

"Therefore do not worry about tomorrow, for tomorrow will worry about itself. Each day has enough trouble of its own."
[6] See the full text of this poem in Appendix 1 - Poems
[7] A Psalm of Life - Henry Wadsworth Longfellow This poem speaks along the same lines of Osler's theme here. See the full poem appendix 1
[8] Paradise Lost - John Milton
[9] Hypochondriacus - Charles Lamb
[10] The Dream of Eugene Aram - Thomas Hood
[11] 1593 – 1633) --Welsh-born English poet, orator and Anglican priest
[12] Genesis 19:26

"But Lot's wife looked back, and she became a pillar of salt."

3

THE LOAD of to-morrow added to that of yesterday, carried to-day, makes the strongest falter. Shut off the future as tightly as the past. No dreams, no visions, no delicious fantasies, no castles in the air, with which, as the old song so truly says, "hearts are broken, heads are turned." To youth, we are told, belongs the future, but the wretched to-morrow that so plagues some of us has no certainty, except through to-day. Who can tell what a day may bring forth? Though its uncertainty is a proverb, a man may carry its secret in the hollow of his hand. Make a pilgrimage to Hades with Ulysses, draw the magic circle, perform the rites, and then ask Tiresias[1] the question. I have heard the answer from his own lips. The future is to-day -- there is no to-morrow! The day of a man's salvation is now -- the life of the present, of to-day, lived earnestly, intently, without a forward-looking thought, is the only insurance for the future. Let the limit of your horizon be a twenty-four hour circle. On the title page of one of the great books of science, the Discours de la Methode of Descartes (1637), is a vignette showing a man digging in a garden with his face towards the earth, on which rays of light are streaming from the heavens; above him is the legend "Fac et Spera"[2] 'Tis a good attitude and a good motto. Look heavenward, if you wish, but never to the horizon -- that way danger lies. Truth is not there, happiness is not there, certainty is not there, but the falsehoods, the frauds, the quackeries, the ignes fatui[3] which have deceived each generation -- all beckon from the horizon, and lure the men not

A Way of Life (Annotated)

content to look for the truth and happiness that tumble out at their feet. Once while at College climb a mountain top, and get a general outlook of the land, and make it the occasion perhaps of that careful examination of yourself, that inquisition which Descartes urges every man to hold once in a lifetime -- not oftener.

Waste of energy, mental distress, nervous worries dog the steps of a man who is anxious about the future. Shut close, then, the great fore and aft bulkheads, and prepare to cultivate the habit of a life of Day-Tight Compartments. Do not be discouraged -- like every other habit, the acquisition takes time, and the way is one you must find for yourselves. I can only give general directions and encouragement, in the hope that while the green years are on your heads, you may have the courage to persist.

[1] A blind Theban seer in Greek mythology. In the Odyssey he kept his gift of prophecy even in the underworld where Odysseus was sent to consult with him.
[2] "Do and hope"
[3] Will-o'-the-wisp: mysterious lights seen by travellers at night, especially over bogs or marshes

4

NOW, FOR the day itself! What first? Be your own daysman[1]! and sigh not with Job for any mysterious intermediary, but prepare to lay your own firm hand upon the helm. Get into touch with the finite, and grasp in full enjoyment that sense of capacity in a machine working smoothly. Join the whole creation of animate things in a deep heartfelt joy that you are alive, that you see the sun, that you are in this glorious earth which nature has made so beautiful, and which is yours to conquer and to enjoy. Realize, in the words of Browning, that "There's a world of capability for joy spread round about us, meant for us, inviting us.[2]" What are the morning sensations? -- for they control the day. Some of us are congenitally unhappy during the early hours; but the young man who feels on awakening that life is a burden or a bore has been neglecting his machine, driving it too hard, stoking the engines too much, or not cleaning out the ashes and clinkers. Or he has been too much with the Lady Nicotine, or fooling with Bacchus[3], or, worst of all, with the younger Aphrodite[4] -- all "messengers of strong prevailment in unhardened youth.[5]" To have a sweet outlook on life you must have a clean body. As I look on the clear-cut, alert, earnest features, and the lithe, active forms of our college men, I sometimes wonder whether or not Socrates and Plato would find the race improved. I am sure they would love to look on such a gathering as this. Make their ideal yours -- the fair mind in the fair body. The one cannot be sweet and clean without the other, and you must realize, with Rabbi

A Way of Life (Annotated)

Ben Ezra,[6] the great truth that flesh and soul are mutually helpful. This morning outlook -- which really makes the day -- is largely a question of a clean machine -- of physical morality in the wide sense of the term. "C'est l'estomac qui fait les heureux,[7]" as Voltaire says; no dyspeptic can have a sane outlook on life; and a man whose bodily functions are impaired has a lowered moral resistance. To keep the body fit is a help in keeping, the mind pure, and the sensations of the first few hours of the day are the best test of its normal state. The clean tongue, the clear head, and the bright eye are birthrights of each day. Just as the late Professor Marsh[8] would diagnose an unknown animal from a single bone, so can the day be predicted from the first waking hour. The start is everything, as you well know, and to make a good start you must feel fit. In the young, sensations of morning slackness come most often from lack of control of the two primal instincts -- biologic habits -- the one concerned with the preservation of the individual, the other with the continuance of the species. Yale students should by this time be models of dietetic propriety, but youth does not always reck the rede[9] of the teacher; and I dare say that here, as elsewhere, careless habits of eating are responsible for mental disability. My own rule of life has been to cut out unsparingly any article of diet that had the bad taste to disagree with me, or to indicate in any way that it had abused the temporary hospitality of the lodging which I had provided. To drink, nowadays, but few students become addicted, but in every large body of men a few are to be found whose incapacity for the day results from the morning clogging of nocturnally-flushed tissues. As moderation is very hard to reach, and as it has been abundantly shown that the best of mental and physical work may be done without alcohol in any form, the safest rule for the young man is that which I am sure most of you follow -- abstinence. A bitter enemy to the bright eye and the clear brain of the early morning is tobacco when smoked to excess, as it is now by a large majority of students. Watch it, test it, and if need be, control it. That befogged, woolly sensation reaching from the forehead to the occiput[10], that haziness of memory, that cold fish-like eye, that furred tongue and last week's taste in the mouth -- too many of you know them -- I know them -- they often come from too much tobacco. The other primal instinct is the heavy burden of the flesh which Nature puts on all of us to ensure a continuation of the species. To drive Plato's team[11] taxes the energies of the best of us. One of the horses is a raging, untamed devil, who can only be brought into subjection by hard fighting and severe training. This much you all know as men; once the bit is between his teeth the black steed Passion will take the white horse Reason with you and the chariot rattling over the rocks to perdition.

With a fresh, sweet body you can start aright without those feelings of inertia that so often, as Goethe says, make the morning's lazy leisure usher in a useless day. Control of the mind as a working machine, the adaptation in it of habit, so that its action becomes almost as automatic as walking, is the end of education -- and yet how rarely reached! It can be accomplished with deliberation and repose, never with hurry and worry. Realize how much time there is, how long the day is. Realize that you have sixteen waking hours, three or four of which at least should be devoted to making a silent conquest of your mental machinery. Concentration, by which is grown gradually the power to wrestle successfully with any subject, is the secret of successful study. No mind however dull can escape the brightness that comes from steady application. There is an old saying, "Youth enjoyeth not, for haste";[12] but worse than this, the failure to cultivate the power of peaceful concentration is the greatest single cause of mental breakdown. Plato pities the young man who started at such a pace that he never reached the goal. One of the saddest of life's tragedies is the wreckage of the career of the young collegian by hurry, hustle, bustle and tension -- the human machine driven day and night, as no sensible fellow would use his motor. Listen to the words of a master in Israel, William James:[13] "Neither the nature nor the amount of our work is accountable for the frequency and severity of our breakdowns, but their cause lies rather in those absurd feelings of hurry and having no time, in that breathlessness and tension; that anxiety of feature and that solicitude of results, that lack of inner harmony and ease, in short, by which the work with us is apt to be accompanied, and from which a European who would do the same work, nine out of ten times, be free." "Es bildet ein Talent sich in der Stille",[14] but it need not be for all day. A few hours out of the sixteen will suffice, only let them be hours of daily dedication -- in routine, in order and in system, and day by day you will gain in power over the mental mechanism, just as the child does over the spinal marrow in walking, or the musician over the nerve centres. Aristotle somewhere says that the student who wins out in the fight must be slow in his movements, with voice deep, and slow speech, and he will not be worried over trifles which make people speak in shrill tones and use rapid movements. Shut close in hour-tight compartments, with the mind directed intensely upon the subject in hand, you will acquire the capacity to do more and more, you will get into training; and once the mental habit is established you are safe

A Way of Life (Annotated)
for life.

Concentration is an art of slow acquisition but little by little the mind is accustomed to habits of slow eating and careful digestion, by which alone you escape the "mental dyspepsy" so graphically described by Lowell[15] in the Fable for Critics.[16] Do not worry your brains about that bugbear Efficiency, which, sought consciously and with effort, is just one of those elusive qualities very apt to be missed. The man's college output is never to be gauged at sight; all the world's coarse thumb and finger may fail to plumb his most effective work, the casting of the mental machinery of self-education, the true preparation for a field larger than the college campus. Four or five hours daily -- it is not much to ask; but one day must tell another, one week certify another, one month bear witness to another of the same story, and you will acquire a habit by which the one-talent man will earn a high interest, and by which the ten-talent man may at least save his capital.

Steady work of this sort gives a man a sane outlook on the world. No corrective so valuable to the weariness, the fever and the fret that are so apt to wring the heart of the young. This is the talisman, as George Herbert[17] says,

> "The famous stone
> That turneth all to gold",[18]

and with which, to the eternally recurring question, What is Life? you answer, I do not think -- I act it; the only philosophy that brings you in contact with its real values and enables you to grasp its hidden meaning. Over the Slough of Despond, past Doubting Castle and Giant Despair, with this talisman you may reach the Delectable Mountains,[19] and those Shepherds of the Mind -- Knowledge, Experience, Watchful and Sincere. Some of you may think this to be a miserable Epicurean doctrine -- no better than that so sweetly sung by Horace:[20] --

> "Happy the man -- and Happy he alone,
> He who can call to-day his own,
> He who secure within can say,
> To-morrow, do thy worst -- for I have
> lived to-day.[21]"

I do not care what you think, I am simply giving you a philosophy of life that I have found helpful in my work, useful in my play. Walt Whitman, whose physician I was for some years, never spoke to me much of his poems, though occasionally he would make a quotation; but I remember late one summer afternoon as we sat in the window of his little house in Camden there passed a group of workmen whom he greeted in his usual friendly way. And then he said: "Ah, the glory of the day's work, whether with hand or brain! I have tried

> "To exalt the present and the real,
> To teach the average man the glory of his
> daily work or trade.[22]"

In this way of life each one of you may learn to drive the straight furrow and so come to the true measure of a man.

[1] An adjudicator, someone who presides, judges and arbitrates during a formal dispute.
[2] Men and Women - The Works of Robert Browning
[3] The Roman god of agriculture and wine. In the Greek pantheon this would be Dionysus.
[4] The Greek goddess of love and beauty.
[5] A Midsummer Night's Dream - William Shakespeare
[6] A poem by Robert Browning. Full text is in the appendix
[7] "It is the stomach that makes people happy,"
[8] Probably referring to Othniel Charles Marsh (October 29, 1831 – March 18, 1899) an American paleontologist who graduated from Yale. From Wikipedia - Marsh was one of the preeminent scientists in the field; the discovery or description of dozens of new species and theories on the origins of birds are among his legacies.
[9] "heed the advice" Perhaps taken from Robert Burns' "Epistle to a Young Friend"
[10] Anatomical term for the back of the head.
[11] Plato's allegory of the charioteer.
"First the charioteer of the human soul drives a pair, and secondly one of the horses is noble and of noble breed, but the other quite the opposite in breed and character. Therefore in our case the driving is necessarily difficult and troublesome."
[12] "Age hath its quiet calm, and youth enjoyeth not for haste." - Martin Farquhar Tupper, Proverbial Philosophy
[13] (1842-1910) American philosopher and psychologist
[14] "Talent develops in silence." - Goethe
[15] James Russell Lowell (1819-1891) American poet, critic, editor and diplomat. Good quote - "The foolish and the dead never change their

A Way of Life (Annotated)
opinions"
[16] From Wikipedia: A Fable for Critics is a book-length poem by American writer James Russell Lowell, first published anonymously in 1848. The poem made fun of well-known poets and critics of the time and brought notoriety to its author.
[17] (1593 – 1633) --Welsh-born English poet, orator and Anglican priest
[18] From "The Elixer" (1633)
[19] The Slough of Despond, Doubting Castle, Giant Despair and the Delectable Mountains are all from "Pilgrim's Progress," a Christian allegory written in 1678 by John Bunyan.
[20] 65 BC - 8 BC -- Roman poet, satirist and critic
[21] The full text of the poem is as follows:

Happy the man, and happy he alone,
He who can call today his own:
He who, secure within, can say,
Tomorrow do thy worst, for I have lived today.   Be fair or foul or rain or shine
The joys I have possessed, in spite of fate, are mine.
Not Heaven itself upon the past has power,
But what has been, has been, and I have had my hour.
--Odes, Book III, xxix. Translation by John Dryden
[22] Song of the Exposition - Leaves of Grass

5

WITH BODY and mind in training, what remains? Do you remember that most touching of all incidents in Christ's ministry, when the anxious ruler Nicodemus came by night, worried lest the things that pertained to his everlasting peace were not a part of his busy and successful life? Christ's message to him is His message to the world -- never more needed than at present: "Ye must be born of the spirit.[1]" You wish to be with the leaders -- as Yale men it is your birthright -- know the great souls that make up the moral radium of the world. You must be born of their spirit, initiated into their fraternity, whether of the spiritually-minded followers of the Nazarene or of that larger company, elect from every nation, seen by St. John.

Begin the day with Christ and His prayer -- you need no other. Creedless, with it you have religion; creed-stuffed, it will leaven any theological dough in which you stick. As the soul is dyed by the thoughts, let no day pass without contact with the best literature of the world. Learn to know your Bible, though not perhaps as your fathers did. In forming character and in shaping conduct, its touch has still its ancient power. Of the kindred of Ram and sons of Elihu, you should know its beauties and its strength. Fifteen or twenty minutes day by day will give you fellowship with the great minds of the race, and little by little as the years pass you extend your friendship with the immortal dead. They will give you faith in your own day. Listen while they speak to you of the fathers. But each age

A Way of Life (Annotated)

has its own spirit and ideas, just as it has its own manners and pleasures. You are right to believe that yours is the best University at its best period. Why should you look back to be shocked at the frowsiness and dullness of the students of the seventies or even of the nineties? And cast no thought forward, lest you reach a period where you and yours will present to your successors the same dowdiness of clothes and times. But while change is the law, certain great ideas flow fresh through the ages, and control us effectually as in the days of Pericles. Mankind, it has been said, is always advancing, man is always the same[2]. The love, hope, fear and faith that make humanity, and the elemental passions of the human heart, remain unchanged, and the secret of inspiration in any literature is the capacity to touch the cord that vibrates in a sympathy that knows nor time nor place.

The quiet life in day-tight compartments will help you to bear your own and others' burdens with a light heart. Pay no heed to the Batrachians[3] who sit croaking idly by the stream. Life is a straight, plain business, and the way is clear, blazed for you by generations of strong men, into whose labours you enter and whose ideals must be your inspiration. In my mind's eye I can see you twenty years hence -- resolute-eyed, broad-headed, smooth-faced men who are in the world to make a success of life; but to whichever of the two great types you belong, whether controlled by emotion or reason, you will need the leaven of their spirit, the only leaven potent enough to avert that only too common Nemesis to which the Psalmist refers: "He gave them their heart's desire, but sent leanness withal into their souls.[4]"

I quoted Dr. Johnson's remark about the trivial things that influence. Perhaps this slight word of mine may help some of you so to number your days that you may apply your hearts unto wisdom.

[1] John 3:1-21
[2] This has been attributed to Goethe.
[3] Frogs or toads
[4] Psalm 106:15

APPENDIX 1 - POEMS

A PSALM OF Life
Henry Wadsworth Longfellow

    Tell me not, in mournful numbers,
    Life is but an empty dream!
    For the soul is dead that slumbers,
    And things are not what they seem.

    Life is real! Life is earnest!
    And the grave is not its goal;
    Dust thou art, to dust returnest,
    Was not spoken of the soul.

    Not enjoyment, and not sorrow,
    Is our destined end or way;
    But to act, that each to-morrow
    Find us farther than to-day.

    Art is long, and Time is fleeting,
    And our hearts, though stout and brave,
    Still, like muffled drums, are beating

A Way of Life (Annotated)
        Funeral marches to the grave.

        In the world's broad field of battle,
        In the bivouac of Life,
        Be not like dumb, driven cattle!
        Be a hero in the strife!

        Trust no Future, howe'er pleasant!
        Let the dead Past bury its dead!
        Act,--act in the living Present!
        Heart within, and God o'erhead!

        Lives of great men all remind us
        We can make our lives sublime,
        And, departing, leave behind us
        Footprints on the sands of time;--

        Footprints, that perhaps another,
        Sailing o'er life's solemn main,
        A forlorn and shipwrecked brother,
        Seeing, shall take heart again.

        Let us, then, be up and doing,
        With a heart for any fate;
        Still achieving, still pursuing,
        Learn to labor and to wait.

RABBI BEN EZRA
Robert Browning

      Grow old along with me!
      The best is yet to be,
      The last of life, for which the first was made:
      Our times are in His hand
      Who saith "A whole I planned,
      Youth shows but half; trust God: see all, nor be afraid!"

      Not that, amassing flowers,
      Youth sighed, "Which rose make ours,
      Which lily leave and then as best recall!"
      Not that, admiring stars,
      It yearned "Nor Jove, nor Mars;
      Mine be some figured flame which blends, transcends them all!"

      Not for such hopes and fears
      Annulling youth's brief years,
      Do I remonstrate: folly wide the mark!

A Way of Life (Annotated)

    Rather I prize the doubt
    Low kinds exist without,
    Finished and finite clods, untroubled by a spark.

    Poor vaunt of life indeed,
    Were man but formed to feed
    On joy, to solely seek and find and feast:
    Such feasting ended, then
    As sure an end to men;
    Irks care the crop-full bird? Frets doubt the maw-crammed beast?

    Rejoice we are allied
    To That which doth provide
    And not partake, effect and not receive!
    A spark disturbs our clod;
    Nearer we hold of God.
    Who gives, than of His tribes that take, I must believe.

    Then, welcome each rebuff
    That turns earth's smoothness rough,
    Each sting that bids nor sit nor stand but go!
    Be our joys three-parts pain!
    Strive, and hold cheap the strain;
    Learn, nor account the pang; dare, never grudge the throe!

    For thence, — a paradox
    Which comforts while it mocks,—
    Shall life succeed in that it seems to fail:
    What I aspired to be,
    And was not, comforts me:
    A brute I might have been, but would not sink i' the scale.

    What is he but a brute
    Whose flesh has soul to suit,

Eddie Merkel

Whose spirit works lest arms and legs want play?
To man, propose this test —
Thy body at its best,
How far can that project thy soul on its lone way?

Yet gifts should prove their use:
I own the Past profuse
Of power each side, perfection every turn:
Eyes, ears took in their dole,
Brain treasured up the whole;
Should not the heart beat once "How good to live and learn?"

Not once beat "Praise be Thine!
I see the whole design,
I, who saw power, see now love perfect too:
Perfect I call Thy plan:
Thanks that I was a man!
Maker, remake, complete, — I trust what Thou shall do!"

For pleasant is this flesh;
Our soul, in its rose-mesh
Pulled ever to the earth, still yearns for rest:
Would we some prize might hold
To match those manifold
Possessions of the brute, — gain most, as we did best!

Let us not always say,
"Spite of this flesh to-day
I strove, made head, gained ground upon the whole!"
As the bird wings and sings,
Let us cry "All good things
Are ours, nor soul helps flesh more, now, than flesh helps soul!"

Therefore I summon age

A Way of Life (Annotated)

    To grant youth's heritage,
    Life's struggle having so far reached its term:
    Thence shall I pass, approved
    A man, for aye removed
    From the developed brute; a God tho' in the germ.

    And I shall thereupon
    Take rest, ere I be gone
    Once more on my adventure brave and new:
    Fearless and unperplexed,
    When I wage battle next,
    What weapons to select, what armour to indue.

    Youth ended, I shall try
    My gain or loss thereby;
    Leave the fire ashes, what survives is gold:
    And I shall weigh the same,
    Give life its praise or blame:
    Young, all lay in dispute; I shall know, being old.

    For, note when evening shuts,
    A certain moment cuts
    The deed off, calls the glory from the gray:
    A whisper from the west
    Shoots — "Add this to the rest,
    Take it and try its worth: here dies another day."

    So, still within this life,
    Tho' lifted o'er its strife,
    Let me discern, compare, pronounce at last,
    "This rage was right i' the main,
    That acquiescence vain:
    The Future I may face now I have proved the Past."

    For more is not reserved

Eddie Merkel

To man, with soul just nerved
To act to-morrow what he learns to-day:
Here, work enough to watch
The Master work, and catch
Hints of the proper craft, tricks of the tool's true play.

As it was better, youth
Should strive, thro' acts uncouth,
Toward making, than repose on aught found made:
So, better, age, exempt
From strife, should know, than tempt
Further. Thou waitedst age: wait death, nor be afraid!

Enough now, if the Right
And Good and Infinite
Be named here, as thou callest thy hand thine own,
With knowledge absolute,
Subject to no dispute
From fools that crowded youth, nor let thee feel alone.

Be there, for once and all,
Severed great minds from small,
Announced to each his station in the Past!
Was I, the world arraigned,
Were they, my soul disdained,
Right? Let age speak the truth and give us peace at last!

Now, who shall arbitrate?
Ten men love what I hate,
Shun what I follow, slight what I receive;
Ten, who in ears and eyes
Match me: we all surmise,
They, this thing, and I, that: whom shall my soul believe?

Not on the vulgar mass

A Way of Life (Annotated)

    Called "work," must sentence pass,
    Things done, that took the eye and had the price;
    O'er which, from level stand,
    The low world laid its hand,
    Found straight way to its mind, could value in a trice:

    But all, the world's coarse thumb
    And finger failed to plumb,
    So passed in making up the main account:
    All instincts immature,
    All purposes unsure,
    That weighed not as his work, yet swelled the man's amount:

    Thoughts hardly to be packed
    Into a narrow act,
    Fancies that broke thro' language and escaped:
    All I could never be,
    All, men ignored in me,
    This, I was worth to God, whose wheel the pitcher shaped.

    Ay, note that Potter's wheel,
    That metaphor! and feel
    Why time spins fast, why passive lies our clay, —
    Thou, to whom fools propound,
    When the wine makes its round,
    "Since life fleets, all is change; the Past gone, seize to-day!"

    Fool! All that is, at all,
    Lasts ever, past recall;
    Earth changes, but thy soul and God stand sure:
    What entered into thee,
    That was, is, and shall be:
    Time's wheel runs back or stops: Potter and clay endure.

    He fixed thee mid this dance

Of plastic circumstance,
This Present, thou forsooth, wouldst fain arrest:
Machinery just meant
To give thy soul its bent,
Try thee and turn thee forth, sufficiently impressed.

What tho' the earlier grooves
Which ran the laughing loves
Around thy base, no longer pause and press?
What tho' about thy rim,
Scull-things in order grim
Grow out, in graver mood, obey the sterner stress?

Look not thou down but up!
To uses of a cup
The festal board, lamp's flash and trumpet's peal,
The new wine's foaming flow,
The Master's lips a-glow!
Thou, heaven's consummate cup, what needst thou with earth's wheel?

But I need, now as then,
Thee, God, who mouldest men!
And since, not even while the whirl was worst,
Did I, — to the wheel of life
With shapes and colours rife,
Bound dizzily, — mistake my end, to slake Thy thirst.

So take and use Thy work,
Amend what flaws may lurk,
What strain o' the stuff, what warpings past the aim!
My times be in Thy hand!
Perfect the cup as planned!
Let age approve of youth, and death complete the same!

THE CHAMBERED NAUTILUS
Oliver Wendell Holmes

> This is the ship of pearl, which, poets feign,
> Sails the unshadowed main,—
> The venturous bark that flings
> On the sweet summer wind its purpled wings
> In gulfs enchanted, where the Siren sings,
> And coral reefs lie bare,
> Where the cold sea-maids rise to sun their streaming hair.
>
> Its webs of living gauze no more unfurl;
> Wrecked is the ship of pearl!
> And every chambered cell,
> Where its dim dreaming life was wont to dwell,
> As the frail tenant shaped his growing shell,
> Before thee lies revealed,—
> Its irised ceiling rent, its sunless crypt unsealed!
>
> Year after year beheld the silent toil
> That spread his lustrous coil;

A Way of Life (Annotated)

    Still, as the spiral grew,
    He left the past year's dwelling for the new,
    Stole with soft step its shining archway through,
    Built up its idle door,
    Stretched in his last-found home, and knew the old no more.

    Thanks for the heavenly message brought by thee,
    Child of the wandering sea,
    Cast from her lap, forlorn!
    From thy dead lips a clearer note is born
    Than ever Triton blew from wreathèd horn!
    While on mine ear it rings,
    Through the deep caves of thought I hear a voice that sings:—

    Build thee more stately mansions, O my soul,
    As the swift seasons roll!
    Leave thy low-vaulted past!
    Let each new temple, nobler than the last,
    Shut thee from heaven with a dome more vast,
    Till thou at length art free,
    Leaving thine outgrown shell by life's unresting sea!

Made in the USA
Lexington, KY
31 October 2017